First Facts®

Transportation Zone

Freight Trains in Action

by Adele D. Richardson

CAPSTONE PRESS
a capstone imprint

First Facts is published by Capstone Press,
151 Good Counsel Drive, P.O. Box 669, Mankato, Minnesota 56002.
www.capstonepub.com

 Books published by Capstone Press are manufactured with paper
containing at least 10 percent post-consumer waste.

Library of Congress Cataloging-in-Publication Data
Richardson, Adele, 1966-
  Freight trains in action / by Adele D. Richardson.
    p. cm. – (First facts. Transportation zone)
  Includes bibliographical references and index.
  ISBN 978-1-4296-6828-6 (library binding)
  1. Railroad trains—Juvenile literature. 2. Freight cars—Juvenile literature.
  3. Railroads—Freight—Juvenile literature. I. Title. II. Series.
  TF148.R526 2012
  625.2—dc22   2011006034

Editorial Credits
Karen L. Daas and Brenda Haugen, editors; Gene Bentdahl, designer; Eric Gohl, media
    researcher; Laura Manthe, production specialist

Image Credits
Alamy/North Wind Picture Archives, 6
Capstone Studio/Karon Dubke, 22
Getty Images Inc./Bloomberg/Jochen Eckel, 17
iStockphoto/Rick Sargeant, 14; zennie, 21
Library of Congress, 10
Newscom/World History Archive, 9
ShutterPoint/Jim Glab, 5
Shutterstock/Bob Orsillo, 13; Brad Sauter, 18; Gary L. Brewer, 1;
    StonePhotos, cover

Printed in the United States of America in North Mankato, Minnesota.

082011   006326R

Table of Contents

Freight Trains...4

Before Freight Trains..7

Inventor of the Locomotive...8

Early Freight Trains..11

Parts of a Freight Train...12

How a Freight Train Works..15

Operating a Freight Train...16

Freight Trains Today..19

Freight Train Facts..20

Hands On: Make Railroad Tracks..............................22

Glossary..23

Read More..24

Internet Sites..24

Index..24

Freight Trains

A whistle blows in the distance. The ground starts to shake. Here comes a freight train! Freight trains move **cargo** from one place to another. Powerful **locomotives** can pull more than 100 cars.

cargo: goods that are carried from one place to another

locomotive: the power unit of a train that pulls cars

Before Freight Trains

Before freight trains were invented, people used horses and wagons to move cargo. Horses struggled to pull heavy loads. Horses could pull loads more easily when the wagons were on rails.

Inventor of the Locomotive

Richard Trevithick built the first locomotive in 1803. Trevithick worked at a coal mine in Wales. This first locomotive pulled coal-filled cars out of the mine. Steam powered the **engine**.

engine: a machine that makes the power needed to move something

Richard Trevithick

Early Freight Trains

The first freight trains used steam-powered locomotives. Train engines burned coal. The hot coal boiled water and made steam. By the 1950s, most freight trains used **diesel** locomotives.

diesel: a type of engine that uses heavy oil that burns to make power

Parts of a Freight Train

Freight trains have different types of cars. **Couplers** hold the cars together. A locomotive pulls the cars. The wheels of the locomotive and cars ride along tracks. Tracks are made up of rails and ties.

coupler: a device at either end of a railroad car that links it to other cars

coupler

wheel

rail

tie

How a Freight Train Works

Most freight trains use diesel engines to power their **generators**. A generator makes electricity to power a motor. The motor turns the wheels of a locomotive. The train's steel wheels ride on two smooth metal rails.

generator: a machine that makes electricity

Operating a Freight Train

An engineer pushes a button to start the train's engine. A **throttle** lever and brake handle control the train's speed. The engineer watches **gauges** to make sure the train is working right.

throttle: a lever that controls how fast a train goes
gauge: a dial that measures something

Freight Trains Today

Different types of freight train cars carry many kinds of cargo. Hoppers carry grain and coal. Tank cars hold liquids. Boxcars carry cargo that must stay dry. Flatcars haul heavy machines. Auto rack carriers haul cars or trucks.

Freight Train Facts

- Workers sort freight train cars in railroad yards. Workers join cars that are going to the same place. Together the cars and a locomotive make up a freight train.

- Freight trains use switches to move from one track to another. These pieces of moveable track guide the freight train's wheels.

- Some freight trains use more than one locomotive. Two locomotives can pull more cars than one can.

Dispatchers make sure trains move safely. Dispatchers watch many trains. They tell engineers which tracks are open for trains. Dispatchers make sure only one train is on a stretch of track at a time.

Hands On: Make Railroad Tracks

A freight train travels smoothly on railroad tracks. You can build model railroad tracks.

What You Need

toy car	craft sticks
a surface such as gravel or sand	glue

What You Do

1. Push your car across gravel or sand.
2. Place four craft sticks side by side in front of you. The sticks should be about 1 inch (2.5 centimeters) apart. The sticks are your ties.
3. Lay two rows of sticks across your ties. The space between the sticks should be equal to the space between the wheels of your car. These are your rails.
4. Glue your rails to your ties. The rails and ties together make your tracks.
5. Place your tracks on the gravel or sand. Push the car over the tracks.

The car moves more smoothly over the tracks than on sand or gravel. There is less friction between the car's wheels and the tracks. Friction is a force that slows down objects when they rub together.

Glossary

cargo (KAR-goh)—goods that are carried from one place to another

coupler (KUHP-lur)—a device at either end of a railroad car that links it to other cars

diesel (DEE-zuhl)—a type of engine that uses heavy oil that burns to make power

engine (EN-juhn)—a machine that makes the power needed to move something

gauge (GAYJ)—a dial that measures something

generator (JEN-eh-ray-ter)—a machine that makes electricity

locomotive (loh-kuh-MOH-tiv)—the power unit of a train that pulls cars

throttle (THROT-uhl)—a lever that controls how fast a train goes

Read More

Hill, Lee Sullivan. *Trains on the Move*. Vroom-Vroom. Minneapolis: Lerner Publications Company, 2011.

Lindeen, Mary. *Trains*. Mighty Machines. Minneapolis: Bellwether Media, 2007.

Shields, Amy. *Trains*. National Geographic Readers. Washington, D.C.: National Geographic, 2011.

Internet Sites

FactHound offers a safe, fun way to find Internet sites related to this book. All of the sites on FactHound have been researched by our staff.

Here's all you do:

Visit *www.facthound.com*

Type in this code: 9781429668286

 Check out projects, games and lots more at **www.capstonekids.com**

Index

cargo, 4, 19
cars, 4, 8, 12, 19, 20
couplers, 12
engines, 8, 11, 15, 16
engineers, 16, 21
generators, 15

locomotives, 4, 8, 11, 12, 15, 20
rails, 7, 12, 15
ties, 12
tracks, 12, 20, 21
Trevithick, Richard, 8